Butterflies and Feathers

Gail Raymond

BookLeaf Publishing

India | USA | UK

Presentation by *BookLeaf Publishing*

Web: www.bookleafpub.com

E-mail: info@bookleafpub.com

ISBN: 9789358317657

First edition 2023

Gone

I was 11 the first time I went numb
The first time the rug was pulled from under me
The first time I realized the world wasn't
sunshine and rainbows
Missed phone call after missed phone call
Where could daddy be?
The worry on mommy's face forced us to think
the worst
It's funny how sometimes even the worst isn't as
bad as the truth
The truth was daddy was gone
But not dead
But dead to us
at least for now

A New Reality

Newspaper headlines, visitation rules, and
collect calls became our new normal
I felt like one of those kids in the movies that
you feel bad for
A broken home, a broken spirit
Everything we thought we knew was gone
Anger, sadness, and hopelessness crept in like
unwelcome visitors
They dropped their luggage and made
themselves at home, deep within my soul while
simultaneously evicting any remaining shreds of
childhood innocence
Forever changed, still numb, alone, and lost

Everyone Needs a Hero

They say not all heroes wear capes
Mine wears jeans and a blouse most days
Daddy was gone, but momma was reborn
I crumbled from the shock, but she rose to the
occasion
She molded me back together, piece by piece
like a fragile work of art
She let the wind dry her tears as she pushed
forward
It didn't matter how little she had, she gave it all
At first I saw a woman who just lost the life she
had always known
Married for almost twenty years to a monster
I was convinced someone would ask to turn our
reality into a movie
I didn't realize then that she lost just what she'd
been praying to lose
She was freed from the hell she'd been living
and he left her the keys to a new life with her
two children
She was free now to be who we needed her to be

Mourning the Living

Learning to mourn the living is a skill not taught
A skill beyond the capabilities of a child
On most days it was burying the pain under a
blanket woven from the fabric of fake smiles
and denial
Other days it was just floating along and hoping
you get where you're going
No one told me it would take decades to master
the art
Every little thing served as a reminder of what
once was
This was the first time I learned life continues
with or without you
Early adolescence dragged me about
Through middle school and high school
Carried along but not a willing participant
I kept my eyes open though
Searching endlessly for something that I couldn't
name
I know now that it was a craving for love and
acceptance
A place to belong
I silently prayed for someone who would accept
me unconditionally and love me endlessly

But like a black cloud always there to remind
me, if daddy could leave-anyone could
No one will stay forever

Mine

The first time we met was a quick run in
He was a friend of a friend
A bad boy, doing young bad boy things
That up to no good smirk, and ocean blue eyes
melted a part of me that was frozen
We were in middle school then, although I had
already been through so much I felt like I'd lived
several lifetimes
Looking back, I was probably obsessed with the
attention
The feeling of having someone say they love
me, even when they didn't have to
Tight hugs and gentle little kisses after school
set my heart on fire
From that moment on he was mine
Through high school, still mine
It didn't matter to me that we hadn't spoken in
years
I knew one day life would place me back in his
arms
They called me crazy, but now they can call me
right

Kismet

Twenty years later, it seems like a dumb idea
Two teenage girls meeting random boys at a
diner and going back to their house for a party
I didn't put much thought into things like that
back then
If it sounded like a good time, I was ready
I was still searching for something
I was still yearning for a place to belong
A bunch of teenagers squished into someone's
bedroom was a typical house party
The party host announced that his cousin would
be stopping by
He arrived and I melted all over again
That same bad boy smile and ocean blue eyes
pierced my soul just as they had when we were
younger
It didn't matter that we hadn't spoken in a few
years
We kissed that night
For hours that didn't seem long enough
It was like our souls were intertwining
Planting a seed that would grow roots deep
within us
We lit a fire that night and it has burned bright
for nearly two decades

I've never had to search again for that feeling,
I found it there at that house party
I sometimes wonder what life would be like if I
didn't go to that party
but I know it was our fate to wind up back in
each other's arms, I believe that with every
ounce of faith I have.

Don't Forget to Remember

The Valentine's Day candy hadn't hardened yet
but something was wrong
Stubborn as a bull, it took a song and dance to
get you to that hospital
You insisted I brush your hair and do your
makeup,
Maybe you knew you weren't coming home
I would've brushed a little longer
A woman with the loudest voice, a booming
laugh
The mouth of a truck driver would echo from
your little 4 foot frame
A woman so full of life, childlike
A kaleidoscope of memories filled with antics
and smiles
Tiny but mighty, we watched as you withered
away
It seemed impossible to imagine a life without
you in it
But seemed selfish to ask you to stay any longer
I sat next to you wondering if you could hear me
I touched up your polish one last time, you were
heading to heaven and knew you needed to look
your best
You weren't scared

You always told me that when God pulled your
number, you looked forward to being reunited
with him
I cringed and winced inside, not knowing what
was coming
"You'll know" the nurse warned us
As your breath sped up, mine slowed
You drifted away, leaving this world behind
With tears in my eyes, a calmness washed over
me
Stillness silenced the room
I never knew death could be so beautiful

Tragedy

The second time I went numb I was sleeping
A 5 a.m. call broke the silence of the night
A frantic panic in my brother's voice that I
hadn't heard in years
He thought I was dead
Instead, I was sleeping peacefully in my bed
Overnight the devil crept in to show me how evil
the world could be
As I was safe at home, death invaded the store I
worked in
Two young lives were cut impossibly short
I thought I was strong
I thought I could deal with loss
Tragic, violent, senseless murder was a dance I
didn't know the steps to
Rumors, gossip, a media circus
It felt like everyone had forgotten that this was
real life
and I was safe at home in my bed

If You Don't Know, Now You Know

The walls closed in around me
I had never experienced pain, confusion, anger,
and sadness in this magnitude
I was shattered in a way I had never been before
I stumbled to my feet, trying to gain some
strength to process the morning's revelations
My bed was empty. Where was he?
My soul was broken and he knew it
I found him cowered under the shower, sobbing
Water crashed over him as he cried tears of relief
For the first time he was forced to imagine a
world without me in it
The thought was too much for either of us
We held each other and wept
And in that moment I realized it didn't matter
how broken I was
He embodied the unconditional love I had
always yearned for
It was him, it had always been him

Moving on

Shadows creep in when you don't have the
strength to move on
If you're lucky, you have someone to carry you
through the darkest days
But even then, you can feel the heaviness
weighing you down
It's true when they say you don't know how
strong you can be until it is your only choice
No one warns you how exhausting being strong
can be
No one mentions the side effects that rear their
ugly head when you least expect it
Or how demoralizing existing just to exist can
be
How rolling with the punches sucks the wind
right out of your lungs
until you wake up one day and realize you're an
unwilling passenger on the roller coaster of life

She Was Gone

This time, he went numb
He stumbled out of bed and peeked in her
bedroom
She was gone
He knew it
He let out a scream
She was gone
The only parent he ever knew
His hero
His model of unconditional love
His home, his heart, his mother
She was gone
His world crashed around him
It was my turn to be the rock
In that moment I felt the emptiness flood his
being
She was gone
He was gone

Rebuilding

We were stuck in a tornado
Eventually the world stopped spinning
We were left to assess the damage
To pick each other up and carry on
We count our blessings everyday that we have
each other
Brick by brick we have laid a foundation that
will not waver
Each loss has taught us that the rain always dries
up
The sun always shines again

Letting It Go

The good thing about experiencing significant
loss is learning to value life
It took so much pain to teach me just how
precious every moment is
I shed the need for anyone's approval
The acceptance I once craved was tucked deep
within my soul
With that came a great inner peace
and just enough room for me to heal the wounds
that had once crippled me

Mourning the Living Part II

I knew I'd get the call one day
"Dad died" my brother told me
It was true, physically he had taken his last
breath
Of course I was sad
The thought of what once was and knowing it
can never be again is always a hard pill to
swallow
But the truth was,
He died long before that moment
The idea of what a father should be
The idea of what I needed him to be
I had learned that sometimes people are
incapable of being what you expect them to be
And it was okay
I was okay
As an adult, I tried to mend that relationship
I gave second chances that I didn't need to
I did all that I could
And it was okay
I was okay

My Happily Ever After

They say fairy tales don't exist in real life
I think that is true but I also think you can come
pretty close
The princess usually faces some turmoil that the
prince saves her from
and they live happily after
I can't say Justin saved me, but we saved each
other
We are each other's happily ever after
As we danced on our wedding day, I pictured
that 12 year old girl
She was broken, scared of what life would bring
She never knew she'd find home in someone's
arms
That one man could be her entire universe
But she knew there was something in that
bad-boy smile and those ocean blue eyes
Staring into those eyes and promising my life,
love, and loyalty until death do us part, was the
happily ever after fairy tales are made of

Dreams

I didn't have a lot of dreams
Sometimes when you are in a constant state of
fight or flight you forget to dream
The only dream I had was to be a teacher
That journey was long
I knew the destination, I had the car, but the road
had twists and turns that I wasn't prepared for
It wasn't until the fear of my dream passing me
by crept in, that I realized it was time to jump
For the first time in my life, jump and not be
afraid of failure
So I closed my eyes and jumped

Falling

The feeling of falling can be exhilarating
Being terrified of the unknown
Not knowing what will happen next
All the things that could send me spiraling into a
full state of panic, I have found beauty in them
I am still falling
I made the decision a few years ago to jump into
anything that terrifies me
I learned that there is joy right on the other side
of fear
There is pride right on the other side of shame
There is hope right on the other side of loss
For too long life was passing me by,
washing me ashore with each passing tide,
I couldn't sit still any longer
Now a willing participant, I continue to fall into
who I'm meant to be

Unwritten

There's so much that is unwritten
Loss that has not been experienced yet
Life that has not been lived
Joy that has not been felt
Tears that have not been cried
That doesn't scare me the way it once did
It just means I'm alive
I'm lucky
I get to write the unwritten